Southern Africa in a Global Context:
Towards a Southern African Security Community

Sam C. Nolutshungu

Southern Africa in a Global Context

Towards a Southern African Security Community

SAPES BOOKS
HARARE

First published 1994
by SAPES Books
P.O. Box MP 111
Mount Pleasant
Harare

Typeset by Southern Africa Printing and Publishing House (SAPPHO) (Pvt) Ltd, 4 Deary Avenue, Belgravia, Harare, Zimbabwe

Cover Design by Hassan Musa

Printed by Print Holdings (Pvt.) Ltd., Harare, Zimbabwe

ISBN 1-77905-021-6

Contents

Southern Africa: Basic Data			
	Population millions (mid-year 1991)	**GNP 1992** millions US$ (constant 1985 prices)	**GDP 1989** millions US$ (constant 1987 prices)
South Africa	38,9	—	87,408
Angola	9,8	9,004	7,466
Botswana	1.3	2,076	1,801
Lesotho	1.8	0,376	0,417
Malawi	8.8	1,305	1,341
Mozambique	16.1	4,491	1,604
Namibia	1.5	1,560	1,710
Swaziland	0.79	0,441	0,636
Tanzania	27.8	9,128	3,741
Zambia	8.6	2,287	2,195
Zimbabwe	10.5	5,002	6,002

Southern Africa in a Global Context: Towards a Southern African Security Community

I. The Global Context

During the Cold War the predominant concern of security studies was the East-West relation seen principally in terms of contingent interstate war involving the United States and the Soviet Union and their respective NATO and Warsaw Pact allies. While conflict and security policy in peripheral regions were not entirely ignored, studies of this kind had little influence on the dominant preoccupations of the field. Similarly, while there were many scholars who stressed the non-military aspects of security, the realist perspective was predominant.[1] The literature on Southern Africa from that period is pretty thin and is mostly about South African policy.[2]

Any attempt to understand the problem of security in Southern Africa today and in the near future, therefore, faces a dual challenge both from the disappearance of the East-West arms race as a straightforward global reference point and from the absence of a well developed tradition of theoretical reflection that encompasses non-military and non-state relations in its conception of security. In addition, the concept of Southern Africa is itself somewhat indeterminate, not only in the sense of which countries it includes, but also in the extent to which it represents a theatre of privileged action for those included and the force of the rational justification of its political demarcation. Quite evidently, the salience of the region as a whole varies markedly among individual states and for each of them there is a definite hierarchy of relevance of members, so far as security is concerned, defined not only by relative power in the region but also by contiguity and past entanglements. It is an empirical question whether the consciousness of ordinary people who are otherwise politically aware incorporates any distinct conception of Southern Africa and whether it has any affective significance for them. There is a danger that behind the reification of region there may be nothing more, in practical terms, than the generation of concepts by the bureaucrats and related intellectuals which merely define the frontiers of expansion of their own activities — a class discourse that is remote from the preoccupations of ordinary people.[3] That makes it all the more important to rescue the concept of security from its narrowly statist uses.

In seeking a broader understanding of 'security' than the narrow one associated with realism, it is necessary, however, to guard against an equally unhelpful tendency which makes "security" encompass all of life's concerns so that its specificity in relation to other areas of reflection and policy is occluded. In the discussion that follows the problem of war is taken as central to the idea of security. War represents a very particular catastrophic contingency matched by very few other phenomena in the range of other forms of insecurity it produces. In the tree of war, clearly, the international is still the most important branch because it is potentially the most destructive and with more far-reaching consequences: whether it takes the form of direct confrontation between states, foreign intervention, proxy wars, or the discrete bankrolling and supply of opposed sides in "civil" conflict. There are, to be sure, other exigencies which are comparable to war in their catastrophic effects which a realistic (if not a *realist*) account must keep in view. For persons and communities, the kind of insecurity we have in mind can be stated no better than, in the language of Alain Joxe, as the threat of death, from war or from hunger.[4] Our principal concern is with that threat as it is produced, not by inadvertence, but by conscious human agency even though we are fully aware that it may be an unintended consequence of policy, or it may, in an ultimate sense, be determined by conditions and situations that are not, themselves, deliberately contrived.

It is a commonplace that most major conflicts that have erupted since the end of the Cold War — with the important exception of the Gulf War of 1991 — have been within states, associated with their break up and the constitution of new ones out of their remains.[5] War is waged among communities and its most poignant feature, whether in Bosnia or in Soweto, is not the movement of well organized military formations and their feats of arms, but atrocious violence against civilians, often committed by civilians as well as elements of regular security forces. States, to be sure, are involved as combatants, as suppliers of arms or as accomplices, but the threat to the order of inter-state relations pales into insignificance beside the insecurity of persons.

Communal strife is by no means new, and present internal wars represent a high point in a trend already well established in the "old" world order.[6] In the Cold War they were assimilated into the East-West conflict, often by recondite ideological or strategic interpretation, while any independent significance for international security they might have tended to be overlooked. While some confrontations were publicly recognized as having a purely internal character, neither side wholly abstained from involvement, which could take many forms and degrees, either direct or through intermediaries. The possibility that the rival power might gain some advantage out of the conflict sustained the interest of the other. Where such balance of power considerations cannot be easily invoked, it is not clear whether a global interest can be defined to motivate action for the resolution of internal conflicts while the absence of global competition may give an intervening power more freedom of action. In this way, the detachment of the Western powers in the face of Russian intervention in Georgia, Armenian in Azerbaijan, Turkish in Iraqi Kurdish areas, reflects less their agreement with the policies of the intervening powers than the lack of a perception of danger to themselves from such military interference. It is very doubtful whether emergent norms and conventions can suffice to motivate powerful states to deal with the predicament of embattled persons and communities where the costs of action to enforce such norms are great, as in Bosnia. Humanitarianism alone, without the backing of self-interest, remains a weak and uncertain master.

The present crises are predominantly internal rather than international, although they are intimately linked to international security in the conventional sense. For, the Cold War operated on certain assumptions of statehood, defending stability in certain areas and impeding national consolidation in others, both by the effect of the convergent interests of the Superpowers in preserving the integrity of some states (as in Eastern Europe and Africa) and by their competitive policies which neutralized each other and, in the end, entrenched the *status quo* (e.g., Korea, Cuba, Israel and Taiwan). The state system which was thus maintained encompassed racial and ethnic orders within states, some of which corresponded to the order of dominance globally, as in the case of white supremacy over blacks in South Africa, while others had no obvious systematic link to international order but were sustained simply to avoid the risks of change.[7] The end of that security order came at the culminating point of a global process of economic retrenchment and restructuring which greatly undermined many political systems and institutions (particulary social movement organizations like e.g., parties and trade unions and their coalitions). The political reforms which have accompanied the economic adjustments globally imposed have yet to prove their capacity to restore political and economic stability. The removal of the Cold War as a security order has unsettled all orders of domination without, in most cases, bringing equality or consensus, either about the ends of politics or its means. Ironically when systems of domination totter, long standing oppositions to them that had a certain coherence and cohesion, that were, indeed, in their way, institutionalized, are apt, in their turn, to be thrown into disarray. On a world scale, the crisis of capitalism was more damaging in the short run to its enemies than to the citadels of private enterprise.

For the Southern African subcontinent — taken here to include Angola, Botswana, Lesotho, Namibia, South Africa, Swaziland, Zambia, Zimbabwe and Tanzania — ramifications of these developments find the point of their concentrated application in South Africa whose fate will profoundly affect the region as a whole for good or ill.[8]

After the Cold War

The changes in the wider world place the liberation of South Africa in an entirely different context than had ever been dreamed in the days when armed national independence movements, one after another, removed the colonial and racist governments of the region. Once inspired by a marxist or fellow travelling nationalism, those movements, now in power or at its threshold, face the fact of the break-up of the Soviet Union and its discredit, succeeded by a Russia with a quite different system of states revolving around it, the collapse of communism all but everywhere and with it, the sustained retreat (or defeat) of the democratic socialist left in the West. In the subcontinent itself old radical voices have become muted, replaced, here and there, by cosmopolitan liberalisms, derivative and strident rather than autochthonous and cerebral, and, for the most part, by an intellectual and ideological void. In economic terms, the era in which the first African independences in the late 1950s and 1960s occurred, which was one of growth and great optimism about development and "catching up" with the industrialized world, has, since the mid-1970s, been followed by recurrent recession in the world and stagnation in Africa, even as the integration of the capitalist world economy has continued apace to falsify and mock African pretensions to economic autonomy and to defining "noncapitalist paths" to development.

Both the Cold War and Soviet power were never as acutely felt in Africa as in other continents, and even when, as it must have appeared to Washington in the 1970s, Soviet arms and influence were sweeping across vast tracts of the continent with the signing of Treaties of Friendship with Ethiopia, Angola and Mozambique, Africa remained firmly in the periphery of East-West conflict — in danger of becoming a theatre of gratuitous intervention and mischief making by Superpowers and their allies who promised a great deal of help in all areas but delivered little, with the Africans themselves exercising no noticeable influence either on the policies of their patrons or on the world at large.

Beleaguered by economic and political problems, African states, in the late 1970s and the 1980s, gradually lost credibility as a collective voice while gestures of independency *vis-a-vis* the Western powers, whether on economic matters, generally, or on such security problems as those of South African aggression, or Chad or Western Sahara, seemed like fits of petulance which were duly rebuked or cheaply appeased. On the one issue that Africans had previously been most influential, the independence of Namibia, their role in the end was little more than one of running errands to SWAPO as constructive engagement proceeded to its ambiguous victory in total disregard of their protests.[9]

Certainly, objective conditions and the correlation of forces, to use some once familiar expressions, played a major part in this enfeeblement and marginalization. But, there was also a lack of leadership and insufficient capacity to act together with consistency and determination on the part of African governments. Governing largely passive populations, unchallenged by effective political opposition, unable to advance beyond the rhetoric and self images of the anticolonial struggle, the governments themselves deteriorated and were singularly unable to produce new ideas, reforms and adjustments to the radically changing international environment.

Despite imperialism and its periodic interventions the Cold War era allowed the new African states a great deal of leeway to attempt solutions of their own and to define their international positions regarding the continent. On the one hand, African states were courted for their votes in the UN and other fora and generally to act as effective echo chambers for the propaganda of each power. On the other, Africa was not critical to the strategic balance or to the major conflicts that punctuated the Cold War, whether in South East Asia or the Middle East. Speculation about what *might* happen if the Soviet Union gained control of Southern Africa or the Red Sea area was fanciful. At the economic level, there was never much competition for the economic resources of the continent which were dependably traded with the West largely by Western expatriate companies in Africa, and in the case of certified countries of socialist orientation, with the help and encouragement of the Soviet Union (for what it was worth).

The importance of African states in the global context was ideological. But ideology exaggerates. It magnified, in African leaders' eyes their own significance in the world (and, ultimately, that of South Africa as well), and some fell "victim to the flattery of the imperialists" (in the language of Simon Kapwepwe). At the same time, the effects of global developments on their own internal conditions were often allowed by sympathetic intellectuals to obscure the opportunities for worthwhile political and economic initiatives at home.[10] Nationalist radicalism which might have been expected to assert creative autonomy degenerated into mere whining and special pleading. Little wonder, then that when Western powers, no longer inhibited by the fear of the rival attraction of the Soviet bloc, inflicted draconian economic reforms on the governments of the continent they all, willy nilly, succumbed and tottered or fell.

Multilateral Hegemony

The complaints of African states are now less audible to the great powers, the economic attraction of the continent, whether for investment or for the expansion of trade, even less important than before. Politically, the focus of the Western powers united in the Group of Seven, to all intents and purposes, is and will remain for a long time the incorporation of Russia and its associated states, the reorganization of Europe, the elimination of what remains of communism in China and its socialization into late capitalism. There is no other pole of power, the illusion of Chinese patronage, once ardently entertained by some movements and states in Southern Africa, can no longer deceive. Though the disappearance of communist resistances to the West in China (and, for that matter everywhere else and, especially in North Korea) may be complicated and slow, it is unlikely that African states will find here an ally for a challenge to Western prescriptions for economy or politics. For the foreseeable future, it is the former Soviet Empire that will be the principal beneficiary of G7 investment, perhaps all the more so as many, with Russia chief among them, are plunged into the most profound social, economic and moral disorder by their abrupt transition.[11]

The security concern of the major powers is concentrated on this area and its immediate periphery in Asia and the Middle East. To these situations Africans can contribute very little, except by providing facilities — communications, air and naval bases that are only occasionally useful — or by a token presence where military action requires world-wide participation or occurs under UN auspices, in the interests of 'diversity'.

Ambitious initiatives by middle level powers in these areas are bound to meet with determined opposition from the US and its allies, so much so that states in those very highly militarized regions might be tempted to look elsewhere to enlarge their global profiles — for whatever domestic or international reasons — and to dump some of their surplus military supplies. A conflict-ridden Africa may appear to offer opportunity in this regard. There is also a danger that, as interest declines in Africa's potential strategic significance for the powers, armed conflict within Africa, even if sustained with foreign arms and money, may go unrestrained. At the same time, the scope for external interference in the continent is much greater, the costs to intervenors being relatively low, a factor, no doubt, behind the occasional suggestions in the West that some African countries should be placed under international government or trusteeship. At a time when it is proving difficult to formulate clear policy for all the internal wars which accompany the birth of the "new world order", Africa's contentions and catastrophes do not appear to be an urgent preoccupation for Western leaders and opinion makers.

US policy remains global and so, in a subordinate and, perhaps, more selective way, are the foreign policies of what it still refers to as "the allies". Yet, a clear picture of what they consider a desirable world order — beyond maintaining the *status quo* — is hard to deduce from the series of *ad hoc* initiatives they have taken since the collapse of world communism. Bold assertion is constrained by the uncertainty of trends of political development around the world and by persistent economic problems at home, but above all, by the absence of a definite enemy of global consequence. The "*status quo*" is provisional but there is every temptation to pretend that it can be stabilized.[12] Consensus is more apparent than real among the dominant countries and profound questions remain about the *raison d'etre* of the alliance, and the proper scope of its commitments and eventual membership.

Nevertheless, some of the preoccupations of US policy are not difficult to infer from what has happened so far. For Washington, it is important to prevent the emergence of any potentially hostile (or noncompliant), military power that can inflict serious damage to US interests in any region of the globe. Nuclear non-proliferation has, accordingly, acquired a greater prominence in US policy as well as the control of the transfer of missile technologies that enlarge the reach of the offensive capacity of middle powers, particularly those suspected of having or planning to develop weapons of mass destruction — like Pakistan. It is supremely important that the offensive nuclear potential of Russia and the Ukraine and the emergent states around them should be curtailed. Related to this aim, but driven by economic considerations as well, there is the desire to consolidate the victory against communism and to ensure a successful and permanent transition to capitalism in Russia and Eastern Europe. The promotion of liberal democracy is seen as furthering both the economic and security interests of the West. Free trade and economic liberalism, associated very strongly with democracy, are pressed on all and sundry. While objectives are set unilaterally, there is a strong commitment to using the UN, now more amenable to US leadership than before, to pursue the policy aims of the US (which, ironically, owes the world body over $1000 million in unpaid subscriptions and contributions to peacekeeping).Underlying this species of multilateralism is an overriding desire to distribute the costs of world order maintenance, as in the war against Saddam Hussein in 1991. Moreover, collective action implies shared responsibility and so eases the burden of legitimating military action that would otherwise be controversial at home. Already overstretched in its peacekeeping operations, the UN has built-in limitations as an instrument of military policy, however. It gives voice and a right of oversight to a wide diversity of countries that are unlikely to agree easily in difficult situations where a common interest is not self-evident.

For the Europeans, privileged association with US military power reduces the pressure for concerted foreign and military policies of their own and makes up for their inability and unwillingness to undertake and pay for the military defence of their various national interests abroad. It remains to be seen, however, whether they can maintain a level of agreement with the US in all important situations comparable to that which obtained during the Cold War. Serious disagreements erupted in the course of 1993 over the proper role for the West in the Balkans and Somalia.

American leadership in the field of security is buttressed by Washington's economic preeminence. Still the largest market and the most innovative, most productive economy, the US has enormous bargaining power *vis-à-vis* all conceivable combinations of advanced economies. Its strength ensures that the role of coordination it assumed at the end of the Second World War can be fulfilled by no other power, while, clearly, none would wish to dispense with it. Leading multilateral hegemony amounts to much more than a position of 'first among equals'. The differences in national economic circumstances among the leading capitalist states produce disagreements about economic policy (e.g., the measure of free trade with the Group of Seven), about the use of economic measures to achieve political aims (as against China for its human rights and missile sales) and about the distribution of the burden of assisting the integration of the former communist world into capitalism. Determined, concerted or explicit opposition to US global policy from advanced industrial states is unlikely, however. Most are satisfied powers who fear other dangers more than American voluntarism.

The very problems they all face, persistent recession and high levels of unemployment favour caution and cooperation rather than bold unilateral moves that might fail. No state can afford to be the first to defect without a realistic prospect of a general reconfiguration of power and interests among the dominant countries.

Notwithstanding, there are still difficulties that cannot be avoided. The first is that hegemony costs. It is by no means clear that an 'equitable' sharing of financial burdens in the exercise of control over the globe can be achieved. Without such cost-sharing, consensus might be hard to realise and the supreme hegemon might be tempted to pursue more provocatively self-centred policies, especially, as its margin of advantage over its partners narrows out of proportion to its assumed hegemonic "responsibilities". The second difficulty is that the cooperative arrangements are vulnerable to internal political developments in the allied countries: all of which have important social problems that compete with defence expenditure and call for conflicting economic solutions, while, so far as public opinion is concerned, they deflate the importance of global management concerns.[13] Third, the composition of the G7 will itself change in time, and its cohesion might be tested as new economic giants emerge outside its charmed circle, with autonomous policies that encourage opposed and competing responses from the original group.

The biggest problem of all is that the world without the Cold War is prone to erupt in regional conflicts that cannot all be given a global significance that makes sense to everyone. This is particularly true of the ethnic conflicts that accompany the emergence of new states.[14] Here, the decisions of world leadership are less clear in their strategic motivation and purposes. The conflicts in Uzbekistan, Tadjikistan and Afghanistan, and the low intensity wars between Armenia and Azerbaijan over ethnic enclaves, and Russia's none too discrete military pressure on Georgia, exploiting ethnic strife, adduce no clear response other than the hope that they will stay limited in scope or fizzle out and, in any case, not upset the apple cart of reform in the former Soviet Union. To be sure, the wisest leadership might amount to doing as little as possible about them, and avoiding military entanglement at all costs. A policy of minimum involvement may also be prudent in other areas of the world like Southern Africa. But, then, it becomes hard to make credible claims for a new world order based on democracy and a regard for international norms, and more difficult to legitimate costly involvement in other crisis areas on such grounds. Consistency is not, however, a decisive criterion of policy or its justification. States in formation, those that are poor, and those that were disadvantaged by the terms on which earlier conflicts were resolved, and those located in the strategic periphery fester for long in disorder and violence without the global order being thereby imperilled.

In a time of change the traditional preference of the major powers for the maintenance of existing state boundaries, which in the past helped the weak states of Africa to survive, is likely to yield to a more changeable response pattern. With "ethnic" and "cultural" interpretations of internal war gaining greater weight on account of the decline of class analysis and struggle all round, notions of ethnic self-determination are likely to gain more acceptance and secessions more sympathy. At the same time, however, none of the norms of good conduct is likely to be consistently upheld. Thus where dictators dig in against the popular will as in Zaire or where would be tyrants reject the results of fair elections as in the case of Savimbi in Angola, and generals in Nigeria, international responses are likely to be weak, favouring any "settlement" that works no matter how remote it may be from the spirit of such norms. Nor does there appear to be any cure for conditions in which electoral processes, perversely enough, return the very same dictators to power whose excesses provoked Western concern in the first place, as, for example, in Kenya and Togo. The reason is that there are no adequate mechanisms at the international level to ensure that the internal development of states conforms to any given principles, and not enough practical reasons of self-interest for any of the powers to exert itself to guarantee such an outcome. Populist appeals to the domestic opinion of the major countries, and especially the US electorate (with a short attention span and impatience with detail when it comes to foreign countries), will, from time to time, be made in response to regional crises: but these are not likely to uphold any intelligible norms.

The doctrines that gain currency in the settlement of disputes in the areas of central strategic importance are likely to be applied to African problems also. Thus, the doctrine of self-determination which was first applied, as we now know tragically, to the very areas of Eastern Europe and the Romanov empire that are now in turmoil, and then used to some effect a quarter of a century later in the UN in support of African decolonization, may now, once again, and just as approximately, be employed to settle, though hardly *solve*, the problem of national integration in Africa by Western governments, by international agencies and by some claimants to power in Africa.[15] There is no way in which the ideologies that emerge out of major conflicts in the world can fail to affect African self-conceptions and political rhetoric.

Whatever the incoherence of a global project of multilateral hegemonic management might be, we may expect continued concentration of trade and investment among the most developed, and even as they reduce trade barriers, more determined efforts to intensify regional economic cooperation as the North American Free Trade Area, the European Community and ASEAN show. Determined Chinese and Japanese economic diplomacy in the Far East and South East Asia indicate a similar regionalism. The structures for North-South cooperation along the lines of associated status with this or that bloc of major trading countries may diminish in importance rather like the British Commonwealth faded away as a framework of significant economic opportunity for its less prosperous members. The possibility of these countries pursuing policies of "de-linking" from world capitalism will be even more fanciful than ever. On the other hand, there is every danger of the world virtually 'de-linking' *de facto* from some of them.

One area of global management that straddles security and economics but in which coherence has still to emerge is that of environmental safety. Beyond the protection of forests and wild animals there are several issues that are both urgent and contentious: the dumping of toxic wastes on countries ill-equipped to handle them, and the controls on pollution in the process of industrialization. Several dimensions of conflict have already become apparent: North-North, North-South, and South-South. Global harmonization of policies may be less easy to achieve, however, than regional agreements among governments and between them and those sections of their populations most affected. NGOs and interest groups of various kinds have stepped into this field with solutions of their own sometimes with far-reaching implications for economic and political policy. The capacity to produce useful controls that respond to specific local needs will depend in large part on the responsiveness of governments to popular interests (which may conflict as between e.g., jobs and clean air, cheap and safe energy, etc.) and on the technological knowledge and alternatives available to them.

Here, another feature in the world system comes into play, namely, the ever widening technological gap between the most prosperous economies and the rest. It helped to undo the Soviet Union economically, but also demonstrated its security implications in the Gulf War. Iraq could muster no effective defence against US missiles while its own weapons were outranged and outsmarted by those of its adversary. That was to be expected. More important was that no other power could produce or dare to supply a country like Iraq the weaponry that had a fighting chance in such a confrontation.

But the technological supremacy of the US and its allies used to great effect by oligopolies of great size that can only be generated by very advanced industrial economies is operative in other spheres as well, and most relevant of all, that of information: not only gathering it with spy satellites and the like (which is probably of no great importance for most African states) but disseminating it through global television. The time may come for many African countries when they may have to abandon even the hope of competing effectively for their national audiences on issues of international interest. By and large this has been true with regard to radio news programs for which significant portions of the elite rely on foreign broadcasts such as those of the BBC and RFI. The challenge of television, however, is on an altogether different scale and its impact on security, especially in times of conflict could be far-reaching, for better or for worse. Given the near impossibility for most countries of closing the technological gap, the challenge will be, while seeking to influence the use of these new instruments of power, to find ways of optimizing the effectiveness of means of communication available to themselves, and enhancing the appeal of their content, to modify this dependence at the level of information, knowledge and ideas, tastes and desires.

The cultural consequences within states and in the region as a whole have important political implications. On the one hand, the constant bombardment with foreign constructions of political and economic reality that is not counterbalanced by effective local and regional communication undermines the possibility of an intelligible, autonomous, internal discourse. Political leaders and their followers are then less capable of understanding and articulating their situation in terms that are authentic to their own experience and appropriate to their capacities and needs. On the other hand, the necessarily disjointed and fragmented way in which the signals are received outside their generative context is mirrored in political consciousness which also lacks coherence and integrity. It becomes difficult to develop an autocentered political culture whether at the national or regional level. A kind of alienation follows. Political identity becomes a matter of external authentication. Thus, for example, foreign perception of conflict in terms of tribal antagonisms, or of certain individuals as sole or authentic representatives of "nations" (e.g., Gatsha Buthelezi and "the Zulu nation"), feed back into local discourse as authoritative even though they contradict political knowledge on the ground. The consequences for the construction of political community and the consolidation of authority are grave. And that is a primary security concern. Media recognition becomes a criterion of international legitimacy, or, at any rate, of inclusion in externally refereed political games whether of negotiation, transition or power sharing.

Norms and Surveillance

The influence of the African continent on all these major changes in the international security environment is small.[16] The critical games are played elsewhere and the continent has little say on the rules or the outcomes. Even so, Africa may be expected to remain a theatre of intermittent external military intervention, whether in the guise of humanitarian action, or to uphold standards of political conduct demanded by Western agencies inter-governmental and non-governmental — superintendents of governance in this periphery of peripheries.

For major states, a double interest sustains this superintendence. Firstly, it establishes a presence which secures dependence and some goodwill especially among beneficiary elites — particularly, intellectuals otherwise mostly superfluous to the needs of their own ruling classes — which is cheap but could turn out to be very useful should it one day happen that the African periphery or its resources increase in strategic or commercial importance. Secondly, it preempts the use of the periphery by other actors as a rear base in their conflicts with the satisfied powers: the anxiety about Iran's role in Sudan is a case in point.

The forces which generate the accretion of superintending agencies, however, reflect more the internal development of the dominant states rather than the realities of the backward areas. The foundations that have sprouted in the US with an aura of altruism as well as ideological usefulness (whether, as before, to protect poor countries from the deceptions and tyranny of communism or, as now, to secure them in the enjoyment of democracy and human rights against big government and authoritarianism), are rooted in a profound capitalist voluntarism: the desire to ensure that private wealth is not appropriated by the state for public purposes. Here, the 'right to choose' where and how to spend private money means the right to determine what worthy causes one will support (if only posthumously), through organizations no less faceless than bureaucracies and a good deal less subject to democratic scrutiny. The voluntarism of the state is matched, with advantage, by private initiative.[17] The explosion of higher education in the humanities and social sciences in the 1960s and 1970s produced a large crop of people who could not be absorbed in government, the military or in business but who could craft a rôle for themselves in the foundations. The Cold War with its need of ambassadors and missionaries in all fields had already prepared the world for these non-governmental non-business activities which acquired an increase of legitimacy in the 1980s when governments neither could nor wished to expand their own efforts in the face of a successful ideological onslaught on big government. There is an affinity between the nationally based NGNBOs (i.e., non-governmental non-business organizations) and Intergovernmental Organizations working in the same fields, the latter additionally sustained by the fact that they provide high level functions for thousands of African expatriates whose countries in economic or political disarray can offer them little that is commensurate with their skills and, dare one say, ambitions.

Assuredly, there are pickings for Africans in the surplus that is vented in this way, yet the crucial decisions, including the high level employment of some of their nationals are decided elsewhere just as more and more of governmental power in their countries is exercised by the helping organizations. Beyond that, poverty imposes the obligation of charity. International assistance, like alms giving whether inspired by the New Testament or the Coran, is a measure of greatness. But it does not abolish need.

The link between security and the activities of NGNBOs is not difficult to show. In 1992 it was widely believed that President Bush took the decision to invade Somalia because of the complaints of humanitarian organizations that were being frustrated in the delivery of food aid by what were simply characterized as warlords and their bands of brigands. While NGNBOs are not all like minded, because they are considered to be disinterested and are of Western provenance, they have an audience in Western decision-making circles that African states can rarely equal. More directly, in times of difficulty they control critical resources — like food — and their distribution. Politically, thanks to the funds they command and the employment opportunities they can offer, they have a power to coopt not only significant numbers of the national intelligentsia but of government functionaries as well. In many cases they also have, admittedly in a haphazard fashion, closer contact with the grassroots on a day to day basis than members of the higher echelons of government in the host countries. For years governments and movements of the Third World (to use another outworn expression), with the memory of Operation Camelot, have been suspicious of them. Yet even without reference to cloak and dagger activities of spies and subversives disguised as NGNBO innocents, there is much here that is relevant to security.

Perhaps, even more than their own activities, the treatment of NGNBO officials within the countries in which they are deployed — their freedom of movement and action and personal safety — has important consequences. Here, again, Somalia may be very instructive. After tens, perhaps, hundreds of thousands of Somalis had perished in fratricidal strife, without provoking 'humanitarian' intervention, the impeding of relief work stung President Bush to intervene and the killing of some two dozen Pakistani soldiers at the service of the UN provoked his successor, President Clinton into helicopter gunship operations redolent of memories of Afghanistan and Vietnam. That is not to say that NGNBOs inherently threaten security; to the contrary, they may also provide vital assistance to it both intentionally and inadvertently in the normal process of the production of knowledge and in helping to meet crises such as those of food 'insecurity'

In a world that is highly integrated, where peoples are interdependent across the boundaries of opulence and misery (for all that they may not know it), the NGNBOs have the potential of speaking up for ordinary people over the heads of their governments, to attract world sympathy and assistance against those regimes if necessary. That is a role that will not be disparaged by those who have been silenced and oppressed by their own governments or communities. However, this service is significantly qualified by the fact that the NGNBOs are themselves part of the structure of inequality and are, ultimately, more responsive to their states and countries of origin than to their hosts.

In Southern Africa , with Angola, Mozambique and South Africa as daily reminders, the problem of war has more to do with the capacity of states to unite populations and to meet armed challenges from internal enemies than with fending off direct external aggression.They are part of the crisis of state formation, arising out of the political and economic conflicts produced by the transformation of racial orders and colonies into new states and from the concomitant emergence of new political forces alongside the dissolution of the solidarities, real and presumed, of the anticolonial and antiracist struggles.

Internal conflicts, to be sure, are fuelled and fanned by external powers, but to an extent that still falls far short of direct external intervention or outright invasion. It is most unlikely that any extraregional state will contemplate a conventional attack on any of the countries in the region in the foreseeable future although armed intervention in civil conflict cannot be ruled out. Within the region itself, as things now stand (with Mozambique and Angola debilitated by war) only three states have the physical capacity to sustain a conventional attack against some of their neighbours: Zimbabwe against Botswana, Tanzania against Zambia, and South Africa against contiguous states. In all cases, except that of a South African attack on one of its immediate neighbours, Lesotho, Botswana, Swaziland or Namibia, the economic, political, and military costs would be so prohibitive that the aggression could not long continue without major external support.

All the conflicts are exacerbated by economic conditions of an extraordinary severity reflecting Africa's historical position in the world economy as well as the contemporary developmental and ecological characteristics of the continent. The low level of real foreign investment in Africa for which official development assistance (overvalued in terms of its magnitude and growth generating effects) and adjustment loans provide no substitute, is the principal cause of poverty and unemployment, both of which generate intractable problems of security. Even the "overdevelopment" of the economic role of the state at the expense of private initiative which it had become fashionable to blame for the poor performance of African economies *before* the Structural Adjustments Policies were adopted, was as much a result as a cause of the low level of private foreign investment in most of the countries of the continent. Indeed, where foreign private companies did operate on any scale before and after independence, they often enjoyed monopoly advantages and state protection. Short of a structural adjustment of the global economy that reorients resources towards the continent and stimulates the exploitation of investment opportunities, states will continue to be unable to prevent the economic marginalization of large sections of their populations and, indeed, whole regions of their national territory, aggravating the already acute problems of national integration.

The countries that have been gripped by persistent civil war — like Chad, Somalia, Liberia and Mozambique — suggest an alarming pattern of response to this continent-wide crisis. As states fail to cope with the demands made upon them, or simply disintegrate, warlordism emerges as a response to the deflation of the economic and political capacity of the state (which it aggravates), and from the very attempts to reconstitute political order. Not only are people stung by their conditions into violence and large numbers of young men made available for armed careers by their unemployment and superfluity in the peacetime economy, but warfare provides a living through plunder and pillage and through the financial assistance from external sympathizers — continuing by other means the predation already associated with the failing states. The periodic peacemaking efforts which often produce a short-lived peace enable these armed formations to adjust their positions in the national economy and their international visibility. Violence is often useful to both ends: the more scandalous it is, the more likely it is to gain media attention and the greater is the gratitude to its perpetrators when they eventually condescend to make peace with their victims. Beyond a certain level of failure, economic life degenerates into plunder, whether in the forms of armed robbery, banditry and warlordism, or the much more common form of corruption which is never innocent of arbitrary coercion and violence.

The security of states within existing boundaries is an ambiguous notion, implying both the security of particular regimes or governments and of the territorial entities over which they rule. Sometimes it is possible to distinguish the government of the day from the state over which it rules, but quite often the process of change itself, while it may not call into question the boundaries of the state, may so undermine the political cohesion of the population which those boundaries enclose such that the state, to all intents and purposes, ceases to function internally even though it continues to exist internationally.[18] That would seem to be the case with Liberia, Somalia, and to a large extent, Sudan as well as the proverbial Chad, and the Mozambican state has not been much more effective since the mid-1980s.

The conventional assumption that when the state (or the regime) is safe its people are also secure must be viewed with some suspicion in the African context, at least, even when we concentrate, as we must do, in the first place, on the physical safety of people, for the following reasons. Few states in Africa, South Africa least of all after the violence of the 1980s and, *a fortiori*, the 1990s, are able to protect effectively more than a small proportion of their population. In some cases, some states cannot be said to be responsive to more than a portion of their people. They then have to sustain themselves by violence and terror. Indeed, in South Africa now, as in Zimbabwe during the 'troubles' in Matabeleland and the membership campaigns of Zanu in the mid-1980s, the state itself is a major source of violence against persons.

To complicate matters even further, the means which sub-Saharan states have at their disposal are of foreign donation, whether they be arms and materiel for armed forces, conventional and unconventional, or the financial backup that makes the prosecution or repulsion of armed violence possible.

The problem of security on the sub-continent is, therefore, one confronting peoples who are not well integrated to their states, and states that are incapable of autonomous self-defence, and, it must follow, independent security *policy.* It is also a problem of contingent dissolution of states and political communities as economic problems, both those of their own making and those imposed by the global economic order into which they are disadvantageously integrated, press with unremitting severity upon them.

In the perspective of state formation, we are bound to regard existing states as provisional, subject, as part of their "emergence", to significant modification in terms of where the international boundaries are drawn as well as in regard to their relation to peoples. That is a security problem to the extent that it carries a potential for internal and external strife. Yet, if the conditions of safety and well being of people dictate different combinations of territory and people or, perhaps, more porous international boundaries and rational qualifications of sovereignty, then, provided these can be achieved peacefully, the process of modification may enhance rather than undermine security.

Southern African countries show signs of growing rather than diminishing external economic dependence. While they can, to some extent, manipulate dependence to their own advantage in building regional cooperation frameworks, like SADC, some doubt must inevitably arise about the measure of autonomy any of the states can enjoy in devising its own defence or in negotiating with the other dependent countries the terms of their common security. Over and above the specific problem of external reliance for arms, extensive economic dependence provokes some scepticism about their scope for independent policy making, and even more about the degree of subjective commitment that policy makers can have to goals set by others for them or which do not depend on their own resources for implementation.

External dependence also affects the ways in which global security problems and roles are defined, and on the rebound, the role of external actors in shaping national and regional security relations. By the same token, international roles in alliances or in multinational organizations, like the UN, raise important questions about the global security framework that would best serve the interests of the region.

During the Cold War, African states did, at a rhetorical level, at least, venture criticism of the global security structure and, as in the Nonaligned Movement, some of them tried conscientiously to loosen the constraints of a bipolar world. Within the continent, through the OAU, they defended the idea of African nonalignment and of a privileged voice and interest for African states in matters affecting states and peoples of the continent. Nonalignment, of course, disappeared with bipolarity while the OAU progressively reflected the disarray of its constituent states, illustrating incidentally, the weakness of

African state initiatives lacking real roots in the political communities they claimed to represent.

With the end of the Cold War all states are either inarticulate or incoherent about security even though one may piece together from state practice in the last five to eight years the emergent ideas of some of the important ones.

For the West, undoubtedly, the new world order is one in which the *status quo* in military power relations is maintained by the forceful suppression of revanchisme and expansionism on the part of any other power; in which moreover, policies of economic management and growth congenial to the West are supported and multiparty democracies attuned to those economic imperatives are promoted. Most regimes in the world, with a lengthening list of exceptions (which includes Cuba, North Korea, Iraq and possibly China, Iran and Sudan, to say nothing of Libya), find safety in affirming that vision of international order and security (though, naturally, not without some cheating).[19]

Problems arise, however, when objective conditions within countries change, creating situations of internal war (that may also spill over to neighbouring states or implicate political movements within those states) or when maverick states behave in deviant ways: then the enforcement of order, or the defence of the *status quo* becomes infinitely more complicated than the mere consensus about it. The same is true when humanitarianism — necessarily always on a selective basis — as in Somalia or Haiti seems to call for robust international enforcement action. Violence strains consensus but it also challenges in the most dramatic ways the principle of non-interference which, for all the breaches in its observance, is the foundation of independent statehood.

Indeed, the enforcement of humanitarian or political standards of conduct by military means is always awkward for states that face the same objective conditions of internal development as the miscreant states, for, they cannot guarantee that they might not themselves be forced into similar deviant behaviour by the dynamics of their own development; for small weak states that can be the object of enforcement but can never, in their turn, enforce anything against the powerful, or oblige the "international community" — reification if ever there was one — to use coercion where they think it appropriate. The conflict between Islamic states and the West over the application of the arms embargo on Bosnian Moslems is a case in point, but so is the paradox of humanitarian UN military action in Somalia but not in Liberia or Angola. The underlying fact which cannot for long be denied is that neither the distribution of coercive capacity nor its control and use, is ever egalitarian or equitable and the interests of peoples, states and groups of states diverge. Resistance is, therefore, assured to any hegemonic project for a new world order.

Southern African Roles

Two questions, then, emerge for states like those of the Southern African region. What international uses of force should they sanction morally, and in which ones should they directly participate; and, how may they ensure either that they do not themselves become the objects of international military action, direct or indirect, or that when such force is applied to their region it is only with their consent and under their influence. Regarding the interests of ordinary people, as distinct from states, it is important to ensure that conventions on the use of force do not protect tyrants or deprive people of their ultimate right of rebellion in the face of misgovernment and the insecurity it breeds. Such concerns would apply with equal, perhaps, even greater force to the security arrangements that may be reached within the region.

Although they can have only a limited impact on situations beyond their own part of the world, Southern African states are challenged to develop and defend considered positions on global security relations and to take part in peacekeeping outside their region. In a general way, they have an interest in the avoidance of war and the pacific settlement of disputes. They may have to consider whether it may not be more advantageous for them to insist on such principles even when the arguments seem compelling for the exemplary enforcement of other norms, as in the Gulf War. For, if they, who are least likely to benefit by such wars or to influence their conduct cannot be the advocates of conciliation, who or what can represent the interests of peace — and order as the antithesis of international violence — in such situations? Similarly, with the special attention that African states have traditionally paid to the UN, they may have to consider whether the present drift from established norms regarding the use of force by the UN which, after Korea, were very restrictive and almost universally judged to be *wisely* so, and from the conventions of peacekeeping which were rigorously intended to avoid war-fighting and partisanship by the UN in civil wars, accord with their own interests. They will need to form a view on how far the UN should become just one more military actor, a surrogate for a superpower, or the military wing of a multilateral hegemonic order, or, even a legitimating chamber for military voluntarism. Finally, in the context of the prevailing agitation for democracy which should, supposedly, inform the "new world order", it would be proper for them to be as responsive, indeed, *obedient,* to their domestic public opinion as the major democracies are to theirs. A striking feature of both the collective action in the Gulf in 1991 and in Somalia in 1993 was the fact that the US government was highly sensitive to *US* polls, while African states, by and large, responded to "principles" and external guidance, with no evident regard for their own public opinion which was very critical of the US-led military action. When bounty hunting was introduced into peacekeeping in Somalia, and while the UN was waging war with tenacity and resolve against one of the parties to the internal conflict, General Farah Aideed was in danger of becoming a folk hero in Africa. In short, it is necessary to ask, in a democratic spirit, what benefit there is to the states and the peoples of the region in the drama of international violence in which they cannot much influence the action or the outcome, or the division of spoils? This is no more than following through on the norm of 'democratic governance' that has been advertized as a feature of the " new world order ".

The principal business of security for Southern African states, however, is their own region, for, it is within this corner of the earth, ravaged by war and civil violence for nearly three decades, that dangers are most likely to arise for people and states. Aggression by extraregional powers against any of the states is unlikely unless it is facilitated, or done by proxy through movements and governments within the region. Admittedly, in a world in which such high levels of integration of military as well as economic systems obtain, the distinction between intraregional and extraregional aggression is a matter of degree, very like the distinction between internal and external war. Nevertheless, it is reasonable to suppose that threats of external aggression are more likely to emanate within the region, i.e., among members of the regional sub-system, if they arise at all, rather than from outside. Although it is difficult to conceive of the circumstances in which any state might wish to launch a conventional attack against any of its neighbours in the absence of serious territorial disputes or irredenta — the recent contention between Botswana and Namibia and the now little mentioned territorial claims of Malawi under Banda notwithstanding — experience shows that the occasions for interstate violence are as numerous as they are unpredictable. In no region can peace be taken for granted. In all cases it needs to be constructed deliberately through structures that sustain and watch over it. The most likely sources of tension and hostility in the sub-continent, however, are most likely to be found in the internal conflicts which the development and consolidation of each new state and society activate and which affect its neighbours in a variety of ways.

The range of possible effects of strife in one country on the security of its neighbours is wide. The interruption of trade and production in countries where, at the best of times, economic life for the majority is at the margin of sufficiency and, for many, well below it, may impose intolerable strains. The creation of refugee populations, themselves insecure, may place enormous social and economic burdens on host communities. It is by no means assured that the traditional, tolerant and receptive attitude of African states towards refugees will continue. Refugees, themselves, can harbour armed movements which envenom relations between the host countries and their home states. Furthermore, sustained conflict in one country may provoke by the force of example or empathy diffusion discontented groups in other countries to resort to similar means. That is where the danger of the present orgy of violence in South Africa lies: it provides a model for alienated elements everywhere in its disdain of both life and death and in its importation of banditry into the very heart of civilization, the city, fusing politics and criminality. In this regard, the proliferation of assault weapons, a legacy of previous wars, and the overspill of arms races in other parts of the globe, together with the existence of marginalized warriors of various hue from that past, are immensely troubling.[20] Very high levels of unemployment and anomie turn many young persons into both the abundant instruments and the superfluous victims of the violence of society.

Political strife in Africa has given impetus to armed criminality as the capacity of states to maintain order diminishes. Personal physical security has become a matter of great urgency for many people. A concept of state or regional security which ignores this reality and its potential would be simply myopic, for not only are acts of brigandage hard to classify exactly between politics and mere crime, but there is not the least doubt that the two elements are in symbiosis in many situations where the state has broken down or is on its way to breaking down. Equally, the magnitude of hardship to which some communities are exposed justify putting this aspect of internal strife on the same plane as the problem of war. It is, however, wise to guard against the sensationalism that seeks to deal with social problems through the rhetoric of war as in the "war against indiscipline" (Nigeria, under Generals Buhari and Idiagbon) or "war against drugs" (US under President Bush) both of which were, in the event, quite ineffectual. What is being highlighted here is the deflation of societies' capacities to deal with crime armed with the weapons of war as a result of war, and the phenomenon of the generation of higher orders of violent criminality as a result of internal war. Both threaten state authority and legitimacy and they reinforce corruption which undermines, at once, good government and economic efficiency.

It is a curious paradox of states in formation, such as those of Southern Africa, that while there is a visible gap in security matters, (more so than in established democracies), between the interests of the state and those of the communities it governs, the state is much more vulnerable to the disorganization of society, even as society in its turn, is more defenceless in the face of the state's violent crises and their consequences: as the experience of Mozambique and Angola, Ethiopia, Somalia, Chad, and Liberia has shown. Both the construction of states and their disintegration are full of the potential for violence, compounded by underdevelopment and the injustices which it breeds.

To summarize: the problems of security that loom largest in the subcontinent are not those of all out war between states, nor, even, in most cases, full blown civil war, though neither can be entirely excluded. What is to be feared is the steady accretion of violent strife and extreme economic necessity which impoverish the quality of political life, undermine economic effort, and aggravate social ills and , for very many people, make life, itself, rather nasty, brutish, and short.[21]

II. A Southern African Security Community

In papers presented at a conference on "Sustainable Peace and Stability" held in Harare at the end of June 1993, two contributors, Jakkie Cilliers and Abdul Minty, approaching the issue from quite different points of view, converged on the need for a Southern African security organization as a means of dealing with the problems and anxieties of the states in the region.[22]

There is a long tradition of cooperation among the major political movements in the region established in the days of the liberation struggle based on a strong belief that the peoples of the various territories faced a common enemy not only in South Africa and its allies, but also in the overall legacy of imperialist domination and underdevelopment. A certain Pan Africanism prevailed in the 1950s and 1960s which, although it seldom embraced the single continental state envisaged by Kwame Nkrumah, nevertheless sought close unity among the peoples and movements of Eastern, Central and Southern Africa which was the major reason for the prodigious sacrifices made by Tanzania and Zambia, and, later Mozambique, in support of the liberation of countries other than their own. In practice, however, movements developed along the lines of nationalisms circumscribed by the boundaries of the colonies in which they were formed. By the late 1960s "liberation in one country" might well have been the slogan of each of the national liberation movements as differences of opportunity, external alignment and ideology eroded the Pan Africanism born of the common experience of European domination.

Within Southern Africa the need for closer economic integration was accepted by all parties and governments however much they might disagree on what it should involve. The Southern Africa Development Coordination Conference set up to gain a measure of independence for the other states *vis-à-vis* South Africa, sought integration among its members even as the Pretoria regime called, variously, for a Southern African Common Market and a sphere of co-prosperity. *De facto*, the economies of the region were articulated to the larger and more developed South African economy in a radial pattern rather reminiscent of the CMEA countries revolving around the Soviet Union. In anticipation of the deracialization of government in South Africa, integration has once again become an important policy issue, with the prospect that in place of the competitive schemes for regional integration, Pretoria's and SADC's, a common framework might emerge.

Liberation movements in the region shared, to some extent, a common political culture, were hosted and aided by the same countries within the region, which were, therefore, exposed to aggression from South Africa. As among independent states, the use of Zimbabwean troops in Mozambique, at the height of the war launched by Renamo with South African help, established a precedent of major security cooperation between governments in power, based as much on Zimbabwe's economic interest in keeping the Beira corridor open as on a sense of solidarity with Frelimo.

Regional cooperation was also realised by the white alliance of Portugal, Rhodesia and South Africa in the 1960s and 1970s, and between various 'dissident' black movements and South Africa in the 1980s in a prodigious effort of destabilization against the newly independent states. While it may be hoped that the extensive networks of subversion established then will disintegrate when South Africa becomes democratic, this is likely to take some time during which some of the elements that fought hard against democracy may try to reconfigure a role for themselves. So far as popular opinion is concerned, it is the universal wish that these individuals and structures be neutralized or swept into the sea. The reality of "national reconciliation" as it has unfolded in Namibia and is in the process of doing in Mozambique and will most likely occur in Angola and South Africa, is that many will remain in the security structures of those countries, for at least a while, with a veil drawn over their deeds of darkness. Zimbabwe set many precedents of 'reconciliation' in this regard and Namibia has added a few.[23]

It is less easy to see how the once opposed networks and traditions of cooperation can be merged in the security field than it is to visualize convergence on economic integration. The challenge will be to achieve sufficient reconciliation so that the antidemocratic elements can be defeated and disarmed, while the new structures, through their democratic legitimacy, deny them fresh political openings among disadvantaged or disaffected populations in the region. To be compatible with legitimacy for the new arrangements and their reliability in the service of popular interests, reconciliation would have to be based on an intelligible ethical foundation.

Whether such standards can be applied, depends on the strength of the democratic forces in each country. In none of them is it likely to be a matter of unilateral decision and, in all cases, the cooperation of external powers will be necessary: including the cessation of encouragement, bankrolling and arming of the undesired elements.

Political deterioration in South Africa could result in the recrudescence of the old terrors in new forms. For South Africa, the question poses itself very directly in relation not only to the torturers and destabilizers still within the security forces, but to their subalterns in the Bantustans and their henchmen in the townships. The problem is compounded by the suspicion which prevails about the role played by the South African Defence Force and the South African Police. Many highly placed officials in Southern Africa are not only deeply conscious of the role these organisations played in regional destabilization but are also convinced of their involvement in the violence in South Africa's townships and in the war UNITA has waged since its electoral defeat. They are certain that De Klerk, presiding over a divided government, and divided in his own mind about relinquishing power, never exercised full control over the Defence Force and many view with considerable scepticism the prospect of the ANC government that is expected to succeed him exercising effective authority over it.

The part played by members of the South African security forces in support of UNITA's war since September 1992, which Pretoria denies but which, like the earlier assistance to Renamo in Mozambique, articulates to a vast international network with at least the secret benevolence if not complicity of several Western governments, reinforces doubt as to the South African security establishment's amenability to democratic change in the region. In a similar way, the South African arms industry — with the same connections as the destabilizers — arouses suspicion as to the interest it may have, for commercial if not ideological reasons, in supplying arms to parties to local conflicts and in helping old customers to positions of power. The establishment of subversion in South Africa is huge, many faceted, and well connected internationally.[24] It straddles the boundaries of government and commerce, of the private and public sectors, and virtually nothing had been done to dismantle it by the time a transitional democratic constitution was agreed in November 1993.

De Klerk's policies during the negotiations were characterized by ambiguities — of conception and of strategy — that contributed greatly to the catastrophic violence against black communities in which some sections of the security forces as well as the Inkatha Freedom Party were prime movers. He has remained ambivalent in his relationship with the extreme white right and solicitous towards the IFP as an essential ally against the ANC. His ambivalent attitude to democracy based on equal votes without racial and ethnic reservations persisted (and had, in fact, to be accommodated in the transitional constitution). On the question of violence, threats of strong action against the culprits went with an over readiness to exonerate the security forces in advance of any proper investigation and at the same time a disavowal of state responsibility for the restoration of law and order — the burden of restoring peace falls on the black leaders. The claim that the South African government with all its resources and with a massive military capability used in the past to devastating effect against black protesters was now unable, rather than unwilling, to curb mass slaughter in the townships strained credulity. If as was sometimes argued, the President could not rely on his forces to implement his policies faithfully, then the fears of the African states would be justified. Yet, even, then, it would be normal to expect in the face of so much carnage — over 10,000 blacks killed in political violence since 1990 — that he would either have admitted failure openly and sought help elsewhere, or held his men to their duty, outfacing rebellion rather than fleeing from the mere possibility of mutiny. Complicity or powerlessness? Neither portends well for the ability of future majority based government to control apartheid's war machine.

Conversions do, however, take place and economic and professional interest together may oblige many to renounce their old ambitions and to adapt themselves to the new political circumstances. De Klerk and his supporters may also, eventually, commit themselves to an unambiguous embrace of political equality as the only stable course and commit its resources fully to making it possible, above all, by suppressing the violence of their own agents and (erstwhile) friends. If, however, the fears expressed regarding the SADF have substance, then, the greater danger would lie not in its attempts to overthrow governments in neighbouring countries, but in the unmanageable security situation that might arise within South Africa itself which would have profound negative consequences for neighbouring countries. The armed forces could, then, not be relied upon to act against right wing subversives or against recalcitrant elements within their own ranks or to react reasonably to militants of the other side. Integration of former apartheid and anti-apartheid forces could be extremely difficult and fraught with the possibility of violence. Unable to rely on the integrated armed forces in the event of need, a future South African government might either have to accept a military veto on its policies (which may not be enough to assure their support or loyalty), or, in the face of, let us say an armed revolt by antidemocratic forces, bring in external forces and brace itself for a sanguinary showdown.

For its part, the SADF sees 'national reconciliation' in terms of elements of the liberation armies of the ANC and the PAC, together with the armies of Transkei, Venda, Bophutatswana and Ciskei being incorporated to itself as an established institution subject to its own criteria of professional suitability. That merely deepens the anxiety of African states that are unconvinced of either the appropriateness of such criteria in a time of fundamental political transformation or the assurance they give about the future conduct of this professional force once renowned for its 'total strategy' of subversion of African regimes.[25]

While no policy of force integration could be guaranteed to work well for a new democracy, it is evident that the model of incorporation into a fundamentally unchanged SADF will not inspire confidence either at home or abroad. At the same time, any restructuring will not succeed without a measure of cooperation from the existing forces of the state. Whatever compromise is struck between radical restructuring and the incorporation model ought to be designed to break up the destabilization networks and to remove known enemies of nonracial democracy from the chain of command. It ought also to ensure that the old units are incapable of operation independently of the new entrants. It might have been expected that a good deal of the preparatory cleansing of the old force should have been undertaken by the old regime once it became convinced of its nonracial, democratic mission. The fact that it was not undertaken in the first three years of the transition merely feeds anxiety. There is a well-founded view that the attitudes of the security services by and large reflect political leadership or its absence.

All the problems of security which have been outlined, as well as the changing international order with its challenges and difficulties argue for collective effort among Southern African states. Regionwide cooperation among governments in the area of security may provide ways of alleviating the problem of force integration. Agreement on the policies that neighbouring states should adopt *vis-a-vis* armed factions in South Africa may foreclose the opportunity for role-seeking adventures in 'soft' neighbouring states or attempts to use them as rear bases for destabilization within the Republic. In a more positive way, raising the debate to a regional level, broadening the number of interlocutors and the range of issues beyond those on which national opinion may be polarized could make a satisfactory agreement more attainable. The process would, in itself, be confidence-building for all concerned. If cooperation were carried to the point of developing regional security institutions it might change the terms of the debate, if only by enhancing career horizons and reinforcing the incentives for cooperation at the national level as well.

Inequality among the states of Southern Africa is a source of suspicion, and there are several that look to the transformation of South Africa with some apprehension in this regard. Even if its internal problems of integration were successfully managed, would a new South Africa be content with a passive role in its region or would it find itself patronizing armed "dissident movements" against neighbours that displeased it? Its economic importance alone assures the Republic a dominant position in the subcontinent, and there may be fears that it may be tempted to use its military power to buttress that advantage. However unfounded such fears may be, given the present state of thinking among those who are likely to succeed the apartheid regime, they may have profound effects on the behaviour of some states.

Great apprehension has been expressed in the region about South Africa's nuclear capability and potential. Still shrouded in secrecy, the projects of the apartheid government in this area raise questions about what the future options of a free South Africa might be. At present, all the parties seem agreed on nuclear disarmament but it is, naturally, unclear what the long term strategic and tactical attraction of nuclear power might be and Southern African states clearly need reassurance on this score. On the other hand, it is most unlikely that such weapons would ever be used within the region. Only in the event of an attack by an extraregional power could their use be invoked, but, then, South Africa would lack the delivery capability which it is most unlikely to develop in the near future.

The size, capacity and disposition of South Africa's conventional forces are a more practical concern but it is unlikely that South Africa could satisfy regional anxieties in this area in the absence of a general understanding on such matters affecting all the countries of the region. Change of military doctrine, as sometimes advocated, from an offensive to a more defensive one would not dispose of the fact that, as things stand, however pacific, a military defence strategy for South Africa would still give it a considerable strike capacity against most of its neighbours. If they should upgrade their own capacities (which they cannot do without considerable external support) they would only encourage apprehension in South Africa and strengthen the hand of those who would want to maintain or build on the Republic's present margin of security. Such an arms race seems difficult to foresee in the practical future but shadows can cause fear and bedevil cooperation which is both necessary and urgent. In the absence of regional agreement and coordination, South Africa's policies on the development and character of its conventional military forces, like those of any other country, is likely to be driven by domestic political considerations, in the absence of any palpable *external* threat and in the face of the massive and complicated *internal* security situation the new state is going to confront.

The prospect of a regional hegemonic role for a black-ruled South Africa, seen against the background of the history of the liberation movement and the potential for radicalism within the black population, will cause unease among major powers and attempts may be made to contain it. There are two ways in which that could be done: one is by encouraging it to dissipate its energy fulfilling flattering but futile intervention roles on the continent or, even further afield (the "Giant of Africa" syndrome); the other is by playing on the fears of its neighbours, to entangle them in external alliances and defence arrangements which symbolize the presence of an external patron. Many people perceive the US construction of an air base in Botswana as ominous in this regard. Such external involvements, breed suspicion and ill-feeling and discourage attempts to build autonomous collective security arrangements. They are likely to be taken to underline the fact that small states have a power of subversion and provocation, particularly, when they believe themselves to be protected by a global hegemon. That is likely to be South Africa's responding anxiety to the apprehensions of its neighbours.

A new South African government may be more sensitive to criticism of its internal performance than to potential military provocations, all the more so if it faces major internal opposition or its political support is weak. The ruling party will also be concerned about maintaining a double image of fidelity to its past *and* of being well adapted to the quite contradictory demands of the present. Utterances by neighbours on such issues may provoke disproportionate anger or gratification that may make cooperation in all areas difficult — either as the result of a peevish irritability which is not uncommon among new states, or a superior disdain of criticism, also a not uncommon response in the continent. Others, too, may tend to be oversensitive to remarks by those close to the new government regarding their policies and actions.

At present, all states, and virtually all movements — with the exception of the far white right in South Africa and its black allies — want to avoid war. At present there are no major interstate disputes in the region and no great ideological cleavages, though suspicion can be magnified, especially where there is a history of past misunderstanding among liberation movements.

Maximizing consultation and joint problem-solving and reducing the negative effects of the region's marginality in the global system require the building of effective regional institutions leading to a well-integrated regional security community, something like NATO but with a radically different orientation that focuses on intraregional problems rather than on external threats. The underlying motives for unity would be to anticipate and avoid conflict, to economize on the costs of securing each state and the region as a whole against it, and to increase the measure of autonomy of the sub-continent in a world system in which it is destined for decades to come to remain weak economically and in terms of its influence on global security.

The existence of shared but heterogeneous security concerns may not have the unifying effect of the presence of an armed ideological opponent with aggressive intentions. Institution building may be more effective in developing such a common awareness than mere analysis and exhortation. The creation of regional institutions could be sustained, even in the absence of an immediately recognized common threat, by a certain bureaucratic momentum and by the palpable economies that can be realized through cooperation in a variety of fields. Integration in the economic sphere would give a tremendous boost to closer cooperation in the area of security also.

Experience shows, however, that agreement on the common interest will not suffice to establish an integrated community if there is no state able and willing to fulfil the role of coordination, mobilizing incentives for cooperation and disincentives for defection. South Africa has the margin of economic advantage to be able to undertake such a role. But coordination is not domination: it is based on consensus and its incentive and disincentive schemes exclude threats of coercion whether military or economic. It rests less on the losses which non-participants are made to incur than on the palpable gains of cooperation.

Whether South Africa would be willing or able in the very near future to fulfil the coordinator role will depend on the evolution of its internal politics. If the present security problems within South Africa are not ameliorated, it will be extremely difficult to focus the attention of government and public opinion on regional issues important and helpful though they might be to the management of internal difficulties. Southern African states, for their part, may be tempted to adopt a wait-and-see attitude so far as institution building is concerned, even as some of them get more entangled in the Republic's problems. The prudent course would be a contrary one, in which they went ahead without the South African state if it was unable to take its part, building on what they have begun to achieve in other areas in SADC, working in close cooperation with the democratic movements in South Africa and the OAU in preparation for the eventual integration of the Republic into a regional security community. It is a fact, however, that security cooperation among SADC members has been patchy and unsystematic despite the important initiatives taken regarding peacemaking in Angola and Mozambique, and its potential barely appreciated by democratic forces inside South Africa. For, if the worst case scenario should materialize — reactionary forces preferring to unleash war rather than submit to democracy — then the goodwill and assistance of the neighbouring states, in denying them rear bases and in funnelling assistance to an embattled democracy, could be of the utmost importance. Although such contingencies are not to be wished for, it is not the business of analysis to wish them away either.

There are numerous areas in which institutions can be built, costs shared and so reduced for individual members. At the level of governments, a ministerial committee or council, meeting with heads of services at regular intervals would be a starting point. Building on existing national resources, a number of structures could be set up quite easily and quickly: e.g., a regional defence college with campuses in different countries, research centres monitoring likely security problems of various kinds, equally decentralized, shared operational facilities, and even a review body on arms production and procurement might go a long way towards concretizing the idea of community.

States may be expected to view with suspicion any idea of security integration which impinges on what they take to be their sovereign prerogatives even if those only amount to the options of external reliance at best, and, at worst, "the right to misgovern ourselves [or, rather, *our people*] as we please."[26] Ruling elites and bureaucratic classes may be expected to cling tenaciously to state nationalism long after the populations (who daily vote with their feet against the constraints of territoriality) have become open to a broader vision. There are, nevertheless, benefits for ordinary people, too, in the autonomy of the states to which they have greater access than they could have to some regional Areopagus. Attempts to transcend sovereignty without first recognizing and giving it full play, merely provoke its obdurate and absurd assertion. Besides, new states place a rather high value on sovereignty and its symbolism. Since they lack real freedom of action in international affairs, their cloud of dignity is held with the weak wind of sovereignty. Time and advantage should, eventually, replace the nationalisms built around arbitrary colonial territorial definitions and permit a larger, more heroic view of the region and its possibilities in the wider world.

Certain principles of relations between states and among peoples would have to gain universal acceptance. In the first instance, states could agree, probably without much difficulty, on the non-use of force and the peaceful settlement of disputes, and on the principle of non-intervention in internal disputes. However, such principles need elaboration and qualification as their application to real situations is not always easy or clear. Above all, a non-interference rule that inherently favours states rather than persons in situations of civil strife would have to be counterbalanced by norms aimed at preventing a regional defence structure from merely becoming a mutual insurance scheme for governments or regimes, and that do allow for the protection of persons in the face of insecurity that may be brought upon them by their own states, and which, on the other hand, also enable states, *in appropriate conditions,* to go to the aid of a member state endangered by internal violence. The only circumstances in which conditions could be deemed appropriate would be where there was consensus on standards of internal political conduct. That presupposes a large measure of political and ideological convergence among the states. If the presently avowed preference for democracy is taken seriously, it should be possible to apply democratic facts to a decision whether the granting or the withholding of aid to an embattled state serves the security of its people as well as those of its regime or state.

Armed intervention, even when it is based on a sure legal and moral foundation, is an extremely hazardous undertaking that rarely achieves a just outcome. Among states that are nearly equal in military capacity it is most unlikely to occur, and if it did would probably do more harm than good. Among unequal states, it would be used against the weak. To err on the side of strict application of a prohibition against armed interference would be more consistent with sovereign equality among states. In cases where there were overwhelming humanitarian grounds to intervene it might be better for that to be done by extraregional agencies, like the UN if the future evolution of that organization and its approach to the use of force were to permit the requisite measure of trust among members of the regional community.

A security community can probably not be achieved without close economic and political cooperation. Agreement has to be possible on a wide range of issues including some that impinge on national sovereignty, such as arms procurement and production with the development of an integrated regional (rather than a merely national, i.e. South African) arms production industry. Extraregional alignments, and particularly, the concession of military facilities to foreign powers are matters on which agreement and mutual assurance will be necessary. Likewise, principles regarding the use of national forces in other countries within the region would have to be multilaterally agreed even if particular decisions, in conformity with such principles, were taken at a bilateral level. In the context of scarce resources, it may also be useful to develop joint training programs and exercises. [27]

The construction of a security community of Southern Africa would be a response to pressing security problems for which there is no more satisfactory solution, but it should also undergird the movement of the region towards closer union in other respects as well. Even if the states of the region are doomed to remain neocolonies in the global economy with little influence on the strategies of great powers, they would still get more out of their peripheral position through unity and cooperation among themselves on those matters that concern them most and which move great powers only intermittently, erratically, and never too deeply.

Political Development

First things last. Integration whether in economic matters or in security is more likely to succeed and endure if the paths of internal political development within the countries of the region do not conflict but converge. Mutual confidence and comprehension are then more likely to be established and the nuisance of "ideological incompatibilities", often wholly factitious or overstated, obviated. The Cold War demonstrated that, as did the revolutionary wars in Europe over a century earlier and their prolonged sequel of strife between democracies and authoritarian states into this century. A substantial measure of convergence of political systems will give peace the best chance.

For now, all major parties in all states affirm a commitment to democracy. Democratization, however, can be protracted, with many twists and turns, while it destabilizes social and economic relations and unleashes strife. The situation of state formation is one of dynamism and turbulence, of fragile regimes and social coalitions, in which institutions always have a provisional character. In such a context what may be more important than the formal options for different systems, or even the formal procedures of periodic more or less competitive elections, is the degree to which the popular forces that can sustain those choices and procedures are strengthened. In a subcontinent where large sections of the population remain illiterate and far removed from the circuits of political influence, democratization means their mobilization and empowerment — not the abandonment of their fate to the mysterious workings of "civil society" in the hope that once interest groups and NGOs are unshackled, they will, *somehow*, build and uphold democracy for all.[28] What is required is the building, expansion and strengthening of *political society* i.e., the capacity of all of society, particularly, its least advantaged strata to acquire an effective voice in politics, a project once half understood by the radical one-party regimes but which needs now to be conceived in a more democratic, anti-authoritarian spirit. The effect of the dominance of the state in postcolonial Africa (always much exaggerated) was a form of depoliticization of society; the proper response to it which is the necessary basis of successful democratization is the *re-politicization* of African societies.

More than just the herding of people into political parties and their involvement in periodic acclamation of charismatic leaders in mass rallies or elections, the construction of political society should deepen popular consciousness of rights and obligations, and of the conditions of their fulfilment locally, nationally and regionally. A sense of political belonging — identity and community — articulated through the various levels of locality, nation and region may then emerge to support the schemes of state construction and cooperation among states and make them more serviceable to the real aspirations of ordinary people. Along these lines, the senses of security as relating to the well-being of regimes and states and as concerning the condition of persons and communities can be brought into closer harmony around a shared ethic of responsiveness and reciprocity among persons and between people and regimes.

Notes

1. Cf Robin Luckham, "Security and Disarmament in Africa" *Alternatives,* 9, Fall 1983; E.A. Kolodziej, "Renaissance in Security Studies? Caveat Lector!" ACDIS Occasional Paper, September 1991, University of Illinois at Urbana Champagne; Laurie Nathan, "The Restructuring and Reorientation of the South African Defence Force" paper presented at the Conference on the theme: "Towards Sustainable Peace and Stability in Southern Africa", Harare, June 30-July 1, 1993.
2. Major studies of the period include J.E.Spence, *The Strategic Significance of Southern Africa,* London, Royal United Services Institution, 1970; K. Grundy, *Soldiers Without Politics; Blacks in the South African Armed Forces,* Berkeley, California, 1983; J. Hanlon, *Beggar Your Neighbours: Apartheid Power in Southern Africa ,* London, Catholic Institute for International Relations, 1986; Scott Jaster, *The Defence of White Power: South African Foreign Policy Under Pressure,* London, Macmillan, 1988.
3. A good deal of group and region-forming in Africa since independence is vulnerable to such criticism every bit as much as the destruction of cross-territorial solidarities from the colonial period responded to the needs of the political classes far more than to any felt need of ordinary people for securely bounded national identities.
4. Alain Joxe, *Voyage aux sources de la guerre,* Paris, Presses Universitaires de France, 1991.
5. Internal strife had been growing steadily around the world long before the end of the Cold War. See, e.g., Ted Gurr, *Minorities at Risk: A Global View of Ethnopolitics,* Washington DC, United States Institute of Peace, 1993.
6. Ted Robert Gurr, *op . cit .,* Ch 4.
7. R. Falk, "Democratising, Internationalising and Globalizing: A Collage of Blurred Images" *Third World Quarterly* 13, 4, 1992 pp 627-640 has some interesting reflections on apartheid and "global apartheid".
8. Tanzania is included largely because of its strong security links in the past with Zimbabwe and Mozambique and for its historical association with the Southern African liberation movements. It is notorious that the boundaries of 'regions' are even more arbitrary than the proverbial African borders.

9. For a controversial account of "constructive engagement" by its chief architect, see Chester Crocker, *High Noon in Southern Africa: Making Peace in a Rough Neighbourhood,* New York, 1992; See also Pauline Baker, *South Africa Time Running Out: The United States and South Africa,* New York, Ford Foundation, 1989.
10. Simon Kapwepwe was one of the most important nationalist leaders of Zambia with Kenneth Kaunda in the United National Independence Party which took power at independence. He used this phrase in criticism of President Kaunda when he broke with him and UNIP to form a short lived opposition party to which Kaunda responded by making Zambia constitutionally a one party state
11. Cf Amnon Kapeliouk, "La grande détresse de la société russe" *Le Monde Diplomatique,* September 1993.
12. Cf Christopher Layne, "The Unipolar Illusion: Why New Great Powers Will Rise" ; Robert Jervis, "International Primacy: Is the Game Worth the Candle?"; and Samuel P. Huntington, "Why International Primacy Matters" all in Sean K. Lynn-Jones and Steven E. Miller, (eds) *The Cold War and After: Prospects for Peace*, Cambridge Mass: MIT Press,1993, pp 244-321.
13. This was shown on a limited scale in Europe in the course of 1993 when problems of recession and inflation led to unilateral responses among Britain, Germany and France leaving the prospects of closer union along the lines envisaged in the Maastricht Treaty much poorer in the wake of dramatic monetary crises for Britain and France. Problems in US relations with the Europeans and with the UN became more public in the autumn of 1993, essentially, arising out of the issue of burden-sharing. See, in particular, Associated Press reports for the 17th, 18th, 20th and 30th October, 1993.
14. Some recent contributions on this subject which underline the policy dilemma include, Gidon Gottlieb, *Nation Against State: A New Approach to Ethnic Conflicts and the Decline of Sovereignty,* New York, Council on Foreign Relations, 1993; Daniel P. Moynihan, *Pandemonium: Ethnicity in International Politics,* Oxford, Oxford University Press, 1993.
15. Cf S. Baynham, "Southern Africa: The Causes and Effects of Regional Instability" pp 13-14, Paper for the Conference "Towards Sustainable Peace and Stability in Southern Africa" Harare, June 30-July 31, 1993. The case for "self-determination" would seem particularly weak on any normative assessment in each of the possible candidate cases considered.
16. For a very valuable discussion of many of the issues raised here see Gilbert M Khadiagala, "Thoughts on Africa and the New World Order", *The Round Table,* 1992, 324, (431-450).
17. See also Sam C. Nolutshungu, "Africa in a World of Democracies: Interpretation and Retrieval" *Journal of Commonwealth and Comparative Politics* Vol XXX No 3, November 1992 pp 316-334.
18. Cf Robert H. Jackson and Carl G. Rosberg, "Sovereignty and Underdevelopment: Juridical Statehood and the African Crisis", *Journal of Modern African Studies* 24; 1 March 1986; see also Brian L. Job (ed), *The Insecurity Dilemma: National Security in the Third World,* Boulder: Lynne Rienner, 1992.

19. For what seem to be likely establishment perceptions, see James G. Blight and Aaron Belkin, "USSR's Third World Orphans: Deterring Desperate Dependents" *Third World Quarterly*, Vol 13 No 4, 1992 pp 715-726.
20. The theme of a major paper by Aristide Zolberg focussed on the displacement of people especially in Africa, prepared for the Social Sciences Research Councils project on the International Security of Marginal Populations.
21. There are some very relevant insights in the essay by F. Eboussi Boulaga, *Les Conférences Naionales en Afrique Noire,* Paris, Editions Karthala, 1993, especially, in his discussion of 'the state of nature' on pp 107 ff.
22. Jakkie Cilliers, "The Future of the South African Arms Industry"; Abdul Minty, "A New Vision of Common Security: From Military Confrontation to Regional Co-operation", papers for the conference, "Towards Sustainable Peace and Stability in Southern Africa", 30 June-2 July 1993.
23. The British born officer, Coventry, who headed the Rhodesian Special Air Services against the nationalists and trained Renamo leader, Dhlakama, was later to fight his erstwhile protegé in Mozambique under Zimbabwean colours. There is, naturally, divided opinion on the merits of such examples of reconciliation, hence the quotation marks.
24. On the ways of what has come to be known as the "third force" see, among many, *Press Conference 11 March 1993, Holiday Inn — Port Elizabeth by Major-General H. B. Holomisa, Chairman of the Military Council of the Republic of Transkei,* Office of the Military Council (1993).
25. Cf. Joseph Hanlon, *Beggar Your Neighbours: Apartheid Power in Southern Africa,* London, Catholic Institute for International Relations, 1986.
26. Without the parenthetical phrase, once a common nationalist retort to colonialists' arguments that Africans were not ready to govern themselves.
27. This shopping list is purely indicative. It is not the purpose of the present discussion to explore all the many practical measures that might be devised.
28. For some useful discussion of "civil society" see Dwayne Woods, "Civil Society in Europe and Africa: Limiting State Power Through a Public Sphere", *African Studies Review,* Vol 35, No 2, September 1992; Adam Seligman, *The Idea of Civil Society,* New York, Free Press, 1992.